Baseball

and the Meaning of Life

Josh Leventhal, Editor

Voyageur Press

Edited by Josh Leventhal
Designed by Maria Friedrich
Printed in China

05   06   07   08   09   5   4   3   2   1

Library of Congress Cataloging-in-Publication Data

Baseball and the meaning of life /
Josh Leventhal, editor.
p. cm.
ISBN-10: 0-89658-712-6 (hardcover)
ISBN-13: 978-0-89658-712-0 (hbk.)
1. Baseball–Quotations, maxims, etc. 2. Baseball
players–Quotations. I. Leventhal, Josh, 1971-
PN6084.B35B35 2005
793.357–dc22
2005009344

Published by Voyageur Press, Inc.
123 North Second Street, P.O. Box 338,
Stillwater, MN 55082 U.S.A.
651-430-2210, fax 651-430-2211
books@voyageurpress.com
www.voyageurpress.com

On the front cover: New York Yankees manager Casey Stengel seeks insight into the future from a crystal (base)ball during Spring Training in 1949.

On the endpapers: Fans enter Boston's Huntington Avenue Baseball Grounds during the 1903 World Series.

On the frontispiece: The catcher's-eye view of fastball from Hall of Fame pitcher Don Drysdale.

On the title page: A game at Chicago's Wrigley Field can be an enlightening experience, such as this Cubs-Cardinals match in May 2004.

Illustration Credits

We wish to acknowledge the following sources for providing the illustrations included in this book. Every effort has been made to locate the copyright holders for materials used, and we apologize for any oversights. Unless otherwise noted, all other illustrations are from the author's collection.

AP/Wide World Photos: front cover, back cover, endpapers, pp. 2, 8, 13, 15, 17, 19, 22, 23, 27, 30, 31, 33–35, 39, 41, 42, 45–47, 49–53, 55, 56, 58–60, 62–65, 67, 68, 72, 73, 75–77, 80, 82–85, 87–89, 91–93, 95, 96.

Photos by Barney Stein: pp. 1, 40, 66.

Library of Congress, Prints & Photographs Division: pp. 11 (FSA/OWI Collection, LC-USF33-005212-M4), 14 (LC-USZ62-94505), 16 (LC-DIG-ppmsca-06616), 18 (LC-USZ62-103763), 26 (LC-DIG-ppmsca-06613), 36 (LC-USZ62-112697), 70 (LC-USZ62-66508).

Royalty-Free/CORBIS: p. 38.

The Elks
Magazine

20 CENTS A COPY

Title Reg. U. S. Pat. Of.

APRIL, 1930

J. F. KERNAN

In This Issue:
WILLIAM G. SHEPHERD has an article for everyone on NATIONAL PROSPERITY

To the Reader

The crack of the bat. The soaring flight of a home run. The smell of freshly cut grass. The taste of cheap beer. All the senses come to life at the ballpark, evoking memories, emotions, and meditations on the meaning of baseball—and the very meaning of life itself.

The classic head-to-head battle between pitcher and batter and the strategic maneuverings of opposing managers have many parallels in our everyday existence. As a result, these games within the game have led the sport's great and not-so-great minds to pontificate on what it all means. The inspirational words of players, managers, umpires, owners, sportswriters, and more are included on the following pages, accompanied by images that bring to life the depths and drama of our national pastime.

Uncle Sam rolls up his sleeves for a time at bat on this *Elks* magazine cover from April 1930.

"Every day is a new opportunity. You can build on yesterday's success or put its failures behind and start over again. That's the way life is, with a new game every day, and that's the way baseball is."

Bob Feller, pitcher

The Pirates and Reds begin a new day, and a new season, at Pittsburgh's home opener in April 2002 at lovely PNC Park.

"I see great things in baseball. It's our game—the American game. It will take our people out-of-doors, fill them with oxygen, give them a larger physical stoicism. Tend to relieve us from being a nervous, dyspeptic set. Repair these losses, and be a blessing to us."

Walt Whitman, writer

Vol. 7.   JUNE, 1902.   No. 3.

PHYSICAL CULTURE 5¢

WEAKNESS A CRIME DON'T BE A CRIMINAL

PHYSICAL CULTURE PUBLISHING CO., Townsend Building, 25th St. and Broadway, NEW YORK, U. S. A.

The cover story in the 1902 issue of *Physical Culture* magazine praised the "Benefits of Ball Games," particularly baseball.

"Whoever wants to know the heart and mind of America had better learn baseball, the rules and realities of the game, and do it by watching first some high school or small-town teams."

Jacques Barzun, writer

A young boy watches a small-town game in Huntingdon, Pennsylvania, in July 1941.

"Baseball gives every American boy a chance to excel, not just to be as good as someone else but to be better than someone else. This is the nature of man, and the name of the game."

Ted Williams, outfielder

The *American Boy* magazine of May 1910 illustrated one boy's efforts to excel at the game of baseball.

"Do what you love to do and give it your very best. Whether it's business or baseball, or the theater, or any field—if you don't love what you're doing and you can't give it your best, get out of it. Life is too short. You'll be an old man before you know it."

Al Lopez, catcher and manager

Ozzie Smith gave it his best for nineteen seasons, and his love of the game was always on display.

13

"Baseball has done more to move America in the right direction than all the professional patriots with all their cheap words."

Monte Irvin, outfielder

With members of the GOP riding the party mascot, Republican and Democratic congressmen head onto the Griffith Stadium field prior to the Capitol Hill baseball match of May 1926.

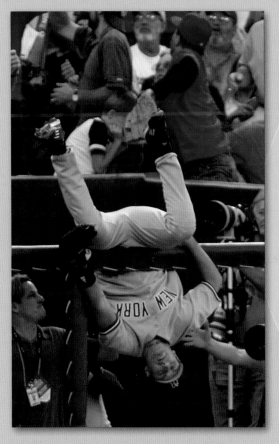

"Baseball is the belly-button of our society. Straighten out baseball, and you straighten out the rest of the world."

Bill "Spaceman" Lee, pitcher

Yankee third baseman Robin Ventura could use some straightening out after chasing a foul ball during the 2002 American League Championship Series.

> **"People ask me what I do in winter when there's no baseball. I'll tell you what I do. I stare out the window and wait for spring."**
>
> *Rogers Hornsby, second baseman and manager*

These Coast Guardsmen don't bother waiting for spring to get in a game of baseball. A stretch of ice in the Bering Sea serves as a playing field for the crew of the icebreaker *Northwind* in 1953.

> "That's the true harbinger of spring, not crocuses or swallows returning to Capistrano, but the sound of a bat on the ball."
> *Bill Veeck, team owner and baseball innovator*

Cincinnati pitchers Brandon Claussen, Paul Wilson, Kent Mercker, and Ricky Stone follow the flight of a pop-up—not swallows at Capistrano—during the first full day of Spring Training in 2005.

> "Baseball is a ballet without music. Drama without words. A carnival without kewpie dolls. Baseball is continuity. Pitch to pitch. Inning to inning. Season to season."
>
> *Ernie Harwell, broadcaster*

A carnival atmosphere reigns at Griffith Stadium as two Washington Senators players clown on the field with a troupe of dancing ladies.

"Baseball is a slow, sluggish game, with frequent and trivial interruptions, offering the spectator many opportunities to reflect at leisure upon the situation on the field. This is what a fan loves most about the game."

Edward Abbey, writer

This lonely spectator reflects in relative solitude upon the situation on the field at Milwaukee's Miller Park in 2002.

"Baseball is like church. Many attend, but few understand."
Wes Westrum, catcher

The two priest-coaches make sure the boys on this seminary baseball team understand both baseball and religion.

"A hot dog at the ballpark is better than a steak at the Ritz."
Humphrey Bogart, actor

OFFICIAL 1967 PHILLIES YEARBOOK
ONE DOLLAR

This young Philadelphia Phillies fan enjoys a ballpark dog slathered with mustard and ketchup.

"I can sit in a ballpark after a game and love looking at the field. Everybody's gone, and the ballpark is empty, and I'll sit there and think, 'Is this as close to heaven as I'm going to get?'"

Kim Braatz-Voisard, centerfielder

The view from the Yankee Stadium upper deck is a little closer than the view from heaven, but the ghosts of past Yankee legends are surely felt in this historic ballpark.

"There is a special sensation in getting good wood on the ball and driving a double down the leftfield line as the crowd in the ballpark rises to its feet and cheers. But I also remember how much fun I had as a skinny, barefoot kid hitting a tennis ball with a broomstick on a quiet, dusty street in Panama."

Rod Carew, infielder

These boys at a Dominican baseball camp hope to someday make the leap from the dusty streets of San Pedro de Macoris to the Major Leagues.

"To play baseball, it's necessary only to have a ball, a bat, a glove, and the imagination of a young boy."

Branch Rickey, team executive

All this young boy needs is some other kids to play with—he appears ready to swing for the fences.

"A team is where a boy can prove his courage on his own. A gang is where a coward goes to hide."

Mickey Mantle, outfielder

The young men on this rough-and-tumble team prepare to prove their courage on the field.

"Sometimes, all of us need to be reminded that this is just a kids' game. We just happen to be grown men playing it."

Mike Stanton, pitcher

A group of youngsters choose up sides for a game on a Major League ball field.

"Baseball was made for kids. Grownups only screw it up."

Bob Lemon, pitcher

Brooklyn's Hall of Fame hurler Dazzy Vance tries to teach a thing or two about pitching to some kids during Spring Training in 1928.

> **"Study and work at the game as if it were a science."**
> *Ty Cobb, outfielder*

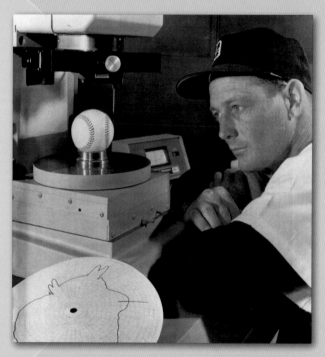

Detroit pitcher Frank Lary studies a brand-new baseball using a Bendix Proficorder, which measures the shape and imperfections of the ball.

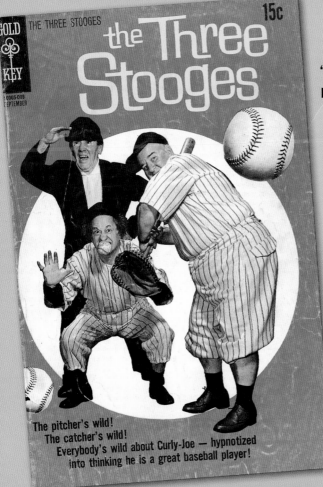

"Slow thinkers are part of the game, too. Some of these slow thinkers can hit a ball a long way."

Alvin Dark, shortstop and manager

These three slow thinkers try their hand at the national pastime in a 1970 comic book—but Curly-Joe is no Joltin' Joe with the bat.

> **"Baseball is like driving. It's the one who gets home safely that counts."**
>
> *Tommy Lasorda, manager*

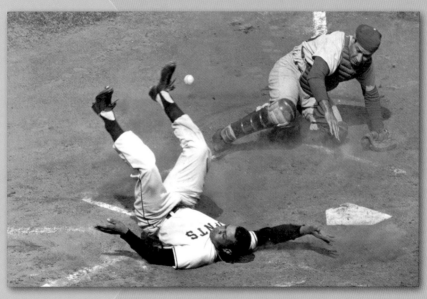

Giants legend Willie Mays gets home safely—barely—after colliding with Phillies catcher Joe Lonnett on an inside-the-park homer at the Polo Grounds in May 1957.

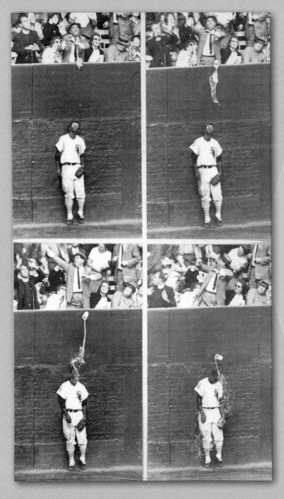

"**Baseball is a lot like life. The line drives are caught, the squibbers go for base hits. It's an unfair game.**"
Ron Kanehl, utility player

White Sox outfielder Al Smith gets a reminder of just how unfair baseball—and life—can be, as he's doused with beer spilled by an eager fan hoping for a souvenir during the 1959 World Series.

"Baseball is almost the only orderly thing in a very unorderly world. If you get three strikes, even the best lawyer in the world can't get you off."

Bill Veeck, team owner and baseball innovator

A pitcher and catcher plead their case to the home-plate umpire on the April 1937 cover of *American Boy*.

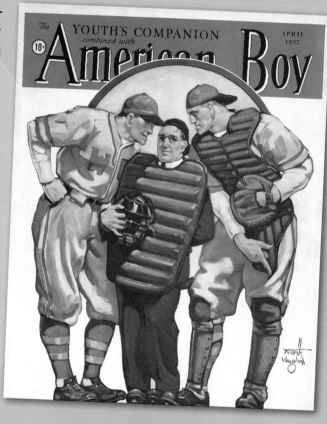

"The game has a cleanness. If you do a good job, the numbers say so. You don't have to ask anyone or play politics. You don't have to wait for reviews."

Sandy Koufax, pitcher

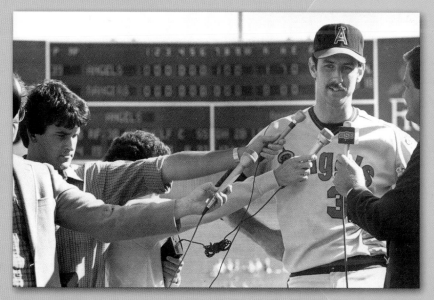

Even with the spotless numbers on the scoreboard, Angels pitcher Mike Witt still has to face the media for reviews after hurling a perfect game on the final day of the 1984 season.

"There's three things you can do in a baseball game: You can win or you can lose or it can rain."

Casey Stengel, manager

An unexpected rain shower hits the town of Surprise, Arizona, delaying a Spring Training game between the Texas Rangers and Kansas City Royals in February 2005.

"Baseball is a game of inches."

Branch Rickey, executive

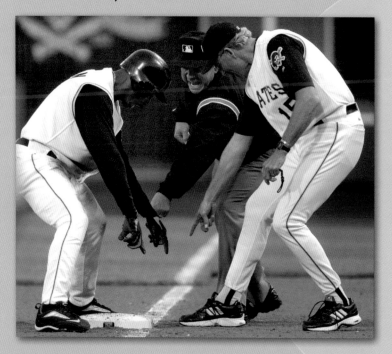

Pirates base-runner Kenny Lofton and coach Rusty Kuntz quibble over inches with umpire Charlie Reliford, who called Lofton out on a pickoff in May 2003.

"I believe in the Rip Van Winkle Theory: that a man from 1910 must be able to wake up after being asleep for seventy years, walk into a ballpark, and understand baseball perfectly."

Bowie Kuhn, Major League Baseball commissioner

American League Park, New York.

This panoramic shows a game at New York's Highland Park on June 8, 1910. The ballpark is long gone, but the rules of the game have changed relatively little since 1910.

"Ninety feet between bases is perhaps as close as man has ever come to perfection."

Red Smith, sportswriter

The baseball diamond has held its now-familiar dimensions for more than a century.

"Changes have been profound and lasting. . . . Exploding score-boards, names on your back, numbers on your front, gloves when you're at bat as well as in the field, and baseball not just under the lights, but under the roof, too, on artificial grass."

Bob Feller, pitcher

Few places demonstrated the sport's profound changes more than the futuristic Astrodome—which Mickey Mantle likened to a flying saucer when it opened in 1965.

"The game has kept faith with the public, maintaining its old admission price for nearly thirty years while other forms of entertainment have doubled and tripled in price. And it will probably never change."

Connie Mack, manager

In the final season at Brooklyn's Ebbets Field in 1957, bleacher seats could be had for seventy-five cents. Today, the cheapest seats at Dodger Stadium in Los Angeles go for six bucks.

"It is ridiculous to pay ballplayers $2,000 a year, especially when the $800 boys often do just as well."

William A. Hulbert, National League president, 1880

Alex Rodriguez smiles broadly after signing a contract with the Texas Rangers that secured him an income of more than $25 million a year for ten years.

"The difference between the old ballplayer and the new ballplayer is the jersey. The old ballplayer cared about the name on the front. The new ballplayer cares about the name on the back."

Steve Garvey, first baseman

Giants shortstop Johnny LeMaster donned the name "Boo" on the back of his jersey in July 1979 in response to persistent jeering from the hometown crowd.

"Everybody thinks of baseball as a sacred cow. When you have the nerve to challenge it, people look down their noses at you. There are a lot of things wrong with a lot of industries. . . . Baseball is one of them."

Curt Flood, outfielder

This cow is anything but sacred to members of the Brooklyn Dodgers at their Spring Training facility in Vero Beach, Florida, in 1950.

> "Any ballplayer that don't sign autographs for little kids ain't an American. He's a communist."
>
> *Rogers Hornsby,*
> *second baseman*
> *and manager*

It's unclear if the top headline on the October 1939 issue of *Liberty* magazine relates to the scene depicted, but this ballplayer is doing his patriotic duty of signing an autograph for an adoring fan.

"I believe we owe something to the people who watch us. When we don't try one hundred percent, we steal from them."

Roberto Clemente, outfielder

Roberto Clemente gives one hundred percent to deny New York's Cleon Jones a base hit in this September 1970 action.

"Don't look back. Something might be gaining on you."
Satchel Paige, pitcher

The Mets' Ricky Henderson looks back to find San Francisco first baseman J. T. Snow gaining on him during a rundown in September 1999. The forty-year-old Henderson was tagged out on the play.

> **"I've seen the future and it's much like the present, only longer."**
>
> *Dan Quisenberry, relief pitcher*

Futuristic spacemen haven't invaded Comiskey Park—it's a group of space-suited midgets hired by Indians owner Bill Veeck for a 1959 stunt.

"You'll never reach second base if you keep one foot on first."

Vernon Law,

The base-runner in this vintage 1910 postcard seems to have no intention of reaching second base.

SAFE
AT FIRST

"Never let the fear of striking out keep you from swinging."

Babe Ruth, outfielder and pitcher

All-time great Mickey Mantle whiffs on one of his 1,710 career strikeouts. On 2,415 other swings, the Mick connected for a base hit.

"You can't be afraid to make errors. No one ever masters baseball or conquers it. You only challenge it."

Lou Brock, outfielder

This error by Boston's Manny Ramirez allowed St. Louis to catch up in the opening game of the 2004 World Series, but Ramirez and the Red Sox bounced back to win the series.

"I don't get upset over things I can't control, because if I can't control them there's no use getting upset. And I don't get upset over the things I can control, because if I can control them there's no use getting upset."

Mickey Rivers, outfielder

Dodgers outfielder Milton Bradley loses control after being ejected from a game in June 2004 for arguing balls and strikes.

> "I never realized that batting a little ball around could cause such commotion."
>
> *Stan Musial, outfielder and first baseman*

New York fans create quite a commotion at Shea Stadium after the "Miracle Mets" upset the Baltimore Orioles to win the 1969 World Series.

"A few million years from now the sun will burn out and lose its gravitational pull. The earth will turn into a giant snowball and be hurled through space. When that happens, it won't matter if I get this guy out."

Bill "Spaceman" Lee, pitcher

The eccentric Bill Lee doesn't seem too concerned about whether the batter is safe or out, as he practices his juggling in the bullpen at Wrigley Field in May 1981.

> "Baseball gives you every chance to be great. Then it puts every pressure on you to prove that you haven't got what it takes. It never takes away that chance and it never eases up on the pressure."

Joe Garagiola,
catcher and
broadcaster

The pressures and thrills of baseball are illustrated on the November 1936 issue of *Thrilling Sports* magazine.

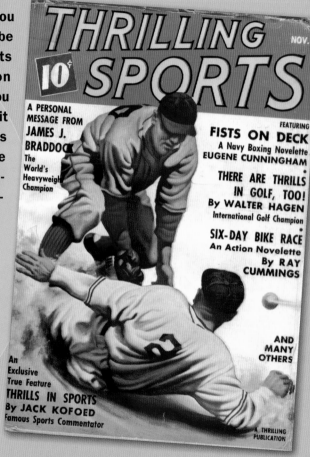

THRILLING SPORTS

NOV.

10¢

A PERSONAL MESSAGE FROM
JAMES J. BRADDOCK
The World's Heavyweight Champion

FEATURING
FISTS ON DECK
A Navy Boxing Novelette
EUGENE CUNNINGHAM

THERE ARE THRILLS IN GOLF, TOO!
By WALTER HAGEN
International Golf Champion

SIX-DAY BIKE RACE
An Action Novelette
By RAY CUMMINGS

AND MANY OTHERS

An Exclusive True Feature
THRILLS IN SPORTS
By JACK KOFOED
Famous Sports Commentator

A THRILLING PUBLICATION

"I'd walk through hell in a gasoline suit to play baseball."

Pete Rose, outfielder and infielder

Pete Rose pours some gas on the fire during the 1973 playoffs between his Reds and the Mets, scuffling with shortstop Bud Harrelson—as a Getty billboard in the background proclaims, "More Gas."

> "You spend a good piece of your life gripping a baseball, and in the end it turns out that it was the other way around all the time."
>
> *Jim Bouton, pitcher and author*

A young Johnny Bench grips seven baseballs in March 1969, before his second full season in the majors.

"Any time you think you have the game conquered, the game will turn around and punch you right in the nose."

Mike Schmidt, third baseman

While Dodgers shortstop Pee Wee Reese may have thought he had the game conquered, he's not actually being punched in the nose by umpire Bill Stewart in this 1949 game action—it's only the camera angle.

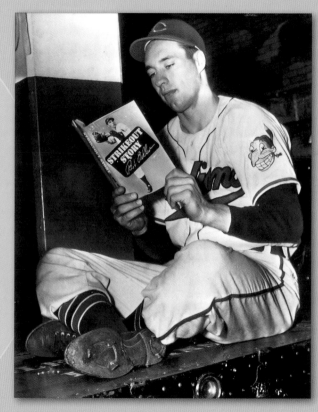

"When you're through learning, you're through."

Vernon Law, pitcher

Bob Feller studies the autobiography of one of the game's greatest pitchers: Bob Feller.

"It's what you learn after you know it all that counts."

Earl Weaver, manager

In his second season as manager of the Washington Senators, Ted Williams makes some adjustments to the batting stance of outfielder Rick Reichardt.

"Age is a case of mind over matter. If you don't mind, it don't matter."

Satchel Paige,
pitcher

The fifty-nine-year-old Satchel Paige pitched three innings for the Kansas City A's in 1965—and offered some helpful lessons to rookie teammate Jim "Catfish" Hunter.

> **"Baseball is a game that allows us to stay young at heart."**
> *Tommy John, pitcher*

Even at the ripe-old age of seventy-eight, A's manager Connie Mack could still swing the bat—at least for a game of pepper with players standing just a few feet away.

> "Baseball is a red-blood-ed sport for red-blooded men. It's no pink tea, and mollycoddles had better stay out. It's a struggle for supremacy, a survival of the fittest."
>
> *Ty Cobb, outfielder*

This struggle for supremacy between the Mets and Cubs in 1996 led to nine player ejections, including Mets reliever John Franco, who had been honored before the game for "John Franco Day."

"Baseball is a game, yes. It is also a business. But what it most truly is, is disguised combat. For all its gentility, its almost leisurely pace, baseball is violence under wraps."

Willie Mays, outfielder

In one of the most violent altercations in Major League history, San Francisco's Juan Marichal takes a bat to the head of Los Angeles catcher John Roseboro during a 1965 game.

> **"The music sounds better, the wine tastes sweeter, and the girls look better when we win."**
>
> *Mark Grace, first baseman*

The girls came out to support the Chicago White Sox during the team's charge to the 1959 American League pennant.

"When you're a winner you're always happy, but if you're happy as a loser you'll always be a loser."

Mark Fidrych, pitcher

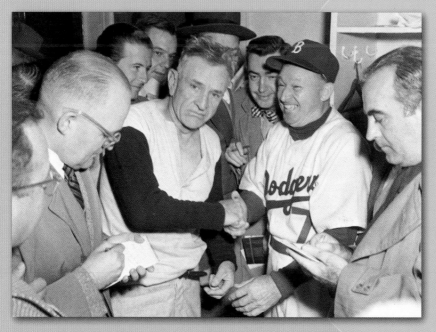

A smiling Chuck Dressen congratulates Casey Stengel after Dressen's Dodgers lost to Stengel's Yanks in the 1952 World Series. The happy Dressen never did win a championship.

> "Grantland Rice, the great sportswriter, once said, 'It's not whether you win or lose, it's how you play the game.' Well, Grantland Rice can go to hell as far as I'm concerned."
>
> *Gene Autry, owner*

You can bet that Dodgers pitcher Ralph Branca shared Gene Autry's assessment after serving up the "shot heard 'round the world" to Bobby Thomson in the 1951 playoff against the Giants.

"If we lose, it will be over my dead body. They'll have to leave me face down on the mound."

Luis Tiant, pitcher

Texas pitcher Francisco Rodriguez lies face down on the mound after getting hit by a line drive in July 2004. Rodriguez lived, but the Rangers lost to the Angels, 11-1.

> "Somebody's gotta win and somebody's gotta lose, and I believe in letting the other guy lose."
>
> *Pete Rose, outfielder and infielder*

Pete Rose made sure the other guy lost in the 1970 All-Star Game, barreling over catcher Ray Fosse to score the game-winning run. Adding injury to insult, Fosse suffered a fractured shoulder on the play.

FRIENDLY FOES

WILLIE McCOVEY • LEON WAGNER

"Buy a steak for a player on another club after the game, but don't even speak to him on the field. Get out there and beat them to death."

Leo Durocher, manager

All-stars Willie McCovey and Leon Wagner share a laugh on the field before facing each other in the 1963 midseason classic.

"What is life, after all, but a challenge? And what better challenge can there be than the one between the pitcher and the hitter."

Warren Spahn, pitcher

In this lithograph from 1870, a pitcher challenges the batter with a pitch and, in the second frame, is struck in the head by the batted ball.

"The pitcher has got only a ball. I've got a bat. So the percentage of weapons is in my favor, and I let the fellow with the ball do the fretting."

Hank Aaron,
outfielder

The number of weapons are not in baseball "clown prince" Johnny Price's favor, but he successfully uses one bat to hit two balls in opposite directions in a pregame exhibition.

"The pitcher has to find out if the hitter is timid. And if the hitter is timid, he has to remind the hitter he's timid."

Don Drysdale, pitcher

Slugger Sammy Sosa gets a refresher course in timidity from Pittsburgh pitcher Salomon Torres, who shattered Sosa's helmet with a fastball to the head in April 2003.

"It helps if the hitter thinks you're a little crazy."
Nolan Ryan, pitcher

With a bloody jersey and blood dripping from his lip, Nolan Ryan might appear crazy in this 1990 photo, but his intensity made him one of the most dominant pitchers of his era.

"**The good Lord was good to me. He gave me a strong body, a good right arm, and a weak mind.**"

Dizzy Dean,
pitcher

Stalled contract negotiations with the Chicago Cubs in 1940 forced Dizzy Dean to slash prices on his good right arm.

"It's called talent. I just have it. I can't explain it. You either have it or you don't."

Barry Bonds, outfielder

Despite allegations that more than talent helped Barry Bonds become the player he was, his dominance of opposing pitchers—as well as his self-confidence—can hardly be questioned.

"It's not the bat that counts. It's the guy who's wielding it."
Paul Waner, outfielder

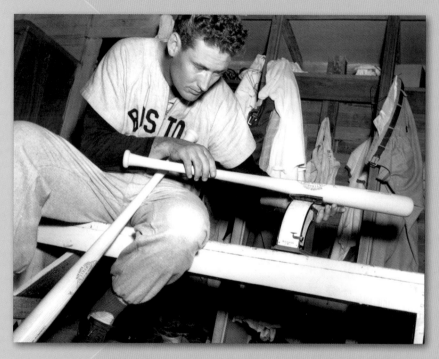

Hitting legend Ted Williams paid a lot of attention to the quality of his bat—and he sure knew how to wield it, too.

"Any baseball is beautiful. No other small package comes as close to the ideal in design and utility. It is a perfect object for a man's hand. Pick it up and it instantly suggests its purpose."

Roger Angell, sportswriter

Apparently, a baseball is a perfect object for a man's mouth, too, at least according to Chicago's Bo Jackson, in May 1993.

"No one can stop a home run. No one can understand what it really is, unless you have felt it in your own hands and body. As the ball makes its high, long arc beyond the playing field, the diamond and the stands suddenly belong to one man. In that brief, brief time, you are free of all demands and complications."

Sadaharu Oh, first baseman

Nobody could stop Bill Mazeroski's dramatic, World Series–winning home run against the Yankees. Pittsburgh's Forbes Field and all of baseball belonged to Maz that October day in 1960.

CINCINNATI REDS YEARBOOK 1967

CROSLEY FIELD

ROSIE REDS

REDS

"ROSIE RED" and "CINCY RED"

PRICE
75
CENTS

-Wiese-

THE FIRST PROFESSIONAL BASEBALL TEAM IN AMERICA—1869

"Chicks dig the long ball."
Greg Maddux and Tom Glavine, pitchers, Nike commercial

"Rosie Red" digs the powerful arms of "Cincy Red" on the cover of the 1967 Reds yearbook.

> **"A catcher and his body are like the outlaw and his horse. He's got to ride that nag till it drops."**
>
> *Johnny Bench,*
> *catcher*

Japan's Tatsuya Suzuki gets an early lesson in the outlaw life of a catcher during the 2001 Little League World Series.

"I worked real hard to learn to play first. In the beginning, I used to make one terrible play a game. Then, I got so I'd make one a week, and finally, I'd pull a real bad one maybe once a month. At the end, I was trying to keep it down to one a season.

Lou Gehrig, first baseman

First baseman Ray Boone works hard, but to no avail, to catch a ball thrown over his head during a 1957 game. The second baseman earned the error here.

"**Second base is anything but magic. If it's anything at all, it's speed, sureness with your hands, and lots of hard work.**"

Nellie Fox, second baseman

Second baseman Red Schoendienst works hard to avoid a collision with Boston base-runner Johnny Pesky during the 1946 World Series.

"The thing that makes a good shortstop is the footwork involved. If you have good footwork, if you can get to the ball, you can set up and get your body out of the way so you can make the throw. I think that's the most important thing."

Larry Bowa, shortstop

Cleveland's Gold Glove shortstop Omar Vizquel uses some fancy footwork to avoid a sliding Paul Molitor and complete the double play in August 1995.

> **"Next to the catcher, the third baseman has to be the dumbest guy out there. You can't have any brains to take those shots all day."**
>
> *Dave Edler,*
> *third baseman*

Detroit's all-star third baseman Travis Fryman takes a shot on a hard grounder in June 1996.

"The test of an outfielder's skill comes when he has to go against the fence to make a catch."

Joe DiMaggio, centerfielder

And when playing in Chicago, the outfielder is tested by vegetation as well. Cubs outfielder Sammy Sosa fights through the Wrigley Field ivy to make a catch at the wall in July 2003.

> "If I ever find a pitcher who has heat, a good curve, and a slider, I might seriously consider marrying him, or at least proposing."
>
> *Sparky Anderson, manager*

Pitcher Bob Feller had it all, but apparently he never got a proposal from manager Ossie Vitt. (In fact, Feller was one of several Cleveland players who tried to get Vitt fired in 1940.)

> **"If you don't have outstanding relief pitching, you might as well piss on the fire and call the dogs."**
>
> *Whitey Herzog, manager*

It seems that the dogs have already been called in San Diego, as Butter the English bulldog hangs out with Padres relievers in the bullpen during Spring Training 2005.

"I believe managing is like holding a dove in your hand. If you hold it too tightly you kill it, but if you hold it too loosely, you lose it."

Tommy Lasorda, manager

There's no dove in manager Casey Stengel's hand during this confrontation with umpire John Flaherty in September 1955—a good thing, because no dove would survive that clenched fist.

"There are three secrets to managing. The first secret is have patience. The second is be patient. And the third most important secret is patience."

Chuck Tanner, manager

Manager Larry Bowa's patience runs thin in June 2003, as he argues a call with umpires Terry Craft and Charlie Reliford. Bowa was ejected from the game.

"The best umpired game is the game in which the fans cannot recall the umpires who worked it. If they don't recognize you, you can enjoy your dinner knowing you did a perfect job."

Bill Klem,
umpire

Apparently misinterpreting the message from the fans, this "Optimistic Umpire" proclaims "Ah, greetings from the boys. It's nice to be remembered." From the October 1926 issue of *Baseball Magazine*.

"I never questioned the integrity of an umpire. Their eyesight, yes."
Leo Durocher, manager

Umpire George Magerkurth has his eyesight and his integrity questioned by the fiery Dodger skipper, Leo "The Lip" Durocher, in April 1946.

"Baseball's a very simple game. All you have to do is sit on your butt, spit tobacco, and nod at the stupid things your manager says."

Bill "Spaceman" Lee, pitcher

Lou Novikoff sits on the bench and keeps quiet during Spring Training with the Los Angeles Angels of the Pacific Coast League in February 1946.

"Baseball must be a great game to survive the fools who run it."
Bill Terry, first baseman and manager

Bud Selig has been running baseball since 1992, during which time the game has survived work stoppages, congressional hearings, and other challenges.

"Some of these guys wear beards to make them look intimidating, but they don't look so tough when they have to deliver the ball. Their abilities and their attitudes don't back up their beards."

Don Drysdale, pitcher

House of David Baseball Team

Drysdale surely wasn't referring to the hirsute House of David barnstorming team, which backed up its beards with a record of 163 wins and 12 losses in 1933.

"The bases were drunk, and I painted the black with my best yakker. But blue squeezed me, and I went full. I came back with my heater, but the stick flares one the other way and the chalk flies for two bases. Three earnies! Next thing I know, skipper hooks me and I'm sipping suds with the clubby."

Ed Lynch, pitcher

Ed Lynch may be the only one who can explain this scene from a Giants-Rockies game in May 1997.

> **"Just when you think you know baseball, you don't."**
>
> *Yogi Berra, catcher*

Marlins outfielders Preston Wilson and Cliff Floyd are at a loss after a ball hit by Cincinnati's Adam Dunn gets lodged in the padding of the outfield wall. It was ruled a ground-rule double.